FOREWORD

IT IS WITH GREAT PLEASURE and humility that I write this foreword for *Radiant Resilience: Unlocking the Secrets to Thriving on Dialysis*. This book will take you on a journey of resilience, hope, and the unwavering spirit that can be found within the depths of the dialysis experience. Being a dialysis patient myself, I truly understand the challenges and complexities that come with this life-altering treatment. It is a path that can often feel isolating, physically demanding, and emotionally draining. However, it is within these trials that we discover incredible strength, a strength that can only be found by those who have walked this path.

What sets this guide apart is its unwavering commitment to staying true to its purpose of supporting you throughout the entire dialysis journey. It includes personal reflection and spiritual practices and emphasizes the powerful influence that faith and belief can have on navigating the highs and lows of dialysis treatment. My hope is that this guide serves as a guiding light for others who are looking for comfort and connection on their journey. Let it guide you in tapping into the well of resilience that lies within each of us.

TABLE OF CONTENTS

INTRO

THE LAST THING ANYONE WANTS to hear from their doctor is that they need to start dialysis. In those shocking initial moments, it can feel like your entire world is crashing down around you as countless questions flood your mind. You're embarking on an unknown journey that requires you to acquire new knowledge, adopt a new lifestyle, and find inner strength—a newfound radiant resilience. My goal with this comprehensive guide is to empower and support both the newly diagnosed and those already on dialysis by providing valuable information, practical advice, and boundless optimism. I want to show you that it is possible to not only survive but also thrive on this journey. Despite the obstacles, living a fulfilling and satisfying life while undergoing dialysis is within reach if you refuse to let it define your life.

I believe you can embrace this stage of your life and find new possibilities with the right attitude, knowledge, and support.

In the following pages, we will explore a wide range of topics together. These topics include managing your physical and emotional well-being, maintaining healthy habits, navigating nutrition restrictions, building a solid support network, and finding joy and purpose in everyday life. Each section has been carefully curated to provide practical strategies, advice from other patients, and daily strategies to better integrate dialysis into a fulfilling life.

I hope this information will empower you to make informed decisions, take control of your health, and live your life to the fullest. Whether you are a dialysis patient, caregiver, or health-care professional seeking insight, this resource is for you.

Remember, thriving on dialysis is not just about physical health. It is also about embracing a positive mindset, pursuing your passions, and finding joy in the present moment. Together, we will set forth on this journey of empowerment and discover the limitless possibilities that lie ahead.

PHYSICAL HEALTH

FOR INDIVIDUALS WITH kidney disease, maintaining physical fitness during dialysis treatment is essential for overall well-being. While dialysis can pose challenges, incorporating regular exercise into your routine offers numerous benefits. Improving cardiovascular health, maintaining weight, and boosting energy levels are crucial for optimizing treatment outcomes. Here are some ways to prioritize your physical fitness:

WALKING: Establishing a regular walking routine, 3-4 times a week, has great benefits for your overall health. In the context of dialysis patients, walking helps increase energy levels, which often get depleted during treatments due to the removal of toxic substances from the body. Regular walking also improves cardiovascular health by reducing blood pressure, enhancing circulation, minimizing the risk of blood clots, and strengthening the heart. This is particularly important, considering that dialysis patients have an increased risk of heart disease. You'll notice after starting this practice that your sessions run a bit smoother, and you lessen the chance of potential cramps or feeling ill after your treatment. Additionally, walking promotes bone health by improving bone density and reducing the risk of fractures or bone-related diseases like osteoporosis. Since dialysis patients are more susceptible to these issues, walking can help prevent their early onset.

WEIGHT MANAGEMENT: You will find fluid retention and nutritional imbalances are common concerns that need to be addressed by dialysis patients. Unfortunately, poor kidney function can lead to fluid retention due to the body's inability to balance fluids. To minimize complications such as edema, fatigue, and stiff joints, it is crucial to maintain a healthy weight and adhere to fluid intake restrictions. Weight and diet also play a significant role in managing high blood pressure. By effectively controlling these factors, patients can regulate their blood pressure and reduce strain on their kidneys and heart. This, in turn, reduces the risk of hospitalization and the need for additional medication. Additionally, following a well-balanced diet and maintaining a healthy weight helps to keep protein, sodium, phosphorus, potassium, glucose, and BUN levels in check, which are closely monitored in laboratory tests.

Consider starting a Diet and Symptom Diary. This diary should record your dietary choices, fluid intake, and any symptoms you experience after treatments. People undergoing dialysis often experience fluctuations in blood pressure and weight, as well as symptoms such as fatigue, dehydration, and gastrointestinal problems. By documenting these factors, you can help your healthcare provider better understand your needs. Additionally, keeping track of symptoms between treatments will make it easier to understand how the treatments are impacting you.

EMOTIONAL WELL-BEING

DIALYSIS IS NOT EASY. It is a challenging process that can lead to feelings of frustration and a loss of control. The demanding nature of treatments, strict dietary restrictions, and lifestyle changes can all contribute to these emotions. Dealing with a chronic illness such as kidney disease and undergoing dialysis treatment can have a significant impact on a patient's emotional health, including leading to feelings of depression, anxiety, and despair. It is crucial to identify and address these emotions to maintain not only your physical but also your mental well-being. Here are some suggestions for maintaining your emotional health:

OPENLY COMMUNICATE: Expressing yourself openly with a trusted friend or family member can empower you and lead to a more positive outlook. Dialysis treatments can often feel monotonous, so it is essential to be proactive during this time. Taking action by ensuring your needs are understood and addressed can alleviate the emotional stress that can come with uncertainty. Your healthcare team is there to support you and to help make the journey less stressful. Dialysis patients tend to be at a higher risk of developing feelings of loneliness and despair, which can impact personal relationships. It is important to be open with your loved ones to maintain a sense of belonging and overcome isolation. Connecting with support groups, mentorship programs, counseling services, and communities specifically designed for dialysis patients can also combat these feelings and allow you to create lasting bonds. Lastly, engaging in creative outlets and participating in activities that bring you joy and promote relaxation can serve as a distraction when times are tough, and it is hard to face another treatment. Remember, when dealing with dialysis, emotional well-being is a journey, so it's important to be kind and patient with yourself.

PRACTICE SELF-CARE: Taking care of yourself is important, but it is even more important for dialysis patients. Many of the restrictions cloud what is possible, and the motivation to perform the basics starts to feel like a burden. A simple way for dialysis patients to practice self-care is by maintaining good hygiene, such as regularly washing their hands, taking care of their skin, and keeping their access points clean. This can help you prevent infections and complications that may require a hospital visit. By performing these tasks, you will find your confidence and self-esteem getting a boost. Another important aspect of self-care is taking medications as prescribed. Dialysis patients often have multiple medications to manage comorbidities, so it is important to take medications as recommended by your healthcare provider. This helps maintain a routine, prevents illnesses, and ensures the effectiveness of treatments. Although self-care may vary depending on individual circumstances, these techniques can have a significant impact when applied properly.

One way to practice self-care is to ensure you are taking medications as directed. One way to streamline this process is with pill organizers. These simple tools are invaluable for ensuring accurate prescription medication adherence. Dedicate a portion of your time each week to organizing your medications according to their prescribed schedule. By forming this habit, you will significantly reduce the chances of missing doses or taking your medications improperly.

Self-care doesn't have to be extravagant, expensive, or trendy. It's a flexible concept that evolves as you progress through treatment and as you navigate your personal journey. It's perfectly acceptable to make adjustments that prioritize your physical, emotional, and mental well-being. Self-care isn't always about adding new products or beauty routines; it can also involve eliminating negative influences like toxic individuals and harmful self-talk, reducing unhealthy snacks, or minimizing excessive screen time. Sometimes, addressing existing obstacles is easier than establishing new routines. Choose what works best for you and honor your path.

MENTAL HEALTH

MENTAL HEALTH ENCOMPASSES our emotional, psychological, and social well-being. It affects our thought patterns, feelings, and how we handle stress-related disruptions in our lives.

Maintaining good mental health is important at every stage of life, but it is especially crucial during the dialysis journey. Prioritizing mental health is essential for patients as they navigate the challenges and adjustments that come with treatment. To improve overall health and quality of life, it is important to take a holistic approach that includes mental health. Here are a few ways to prioritize your mental health:

LIMITING NEGATIVE INFLUENCES: Minimizing or avoiding factors that negatively impact well-being is referred to as limiting negative influences. This involves being mindful of people, environments, and activities that can contribute to your negative emotions, stress, and unhealthy behaviors. Creating a healthy and positive environment is crucial for dialysis patients. Feelings of depression, thoughts of mortality, anxiety, and despondency are more common during this time, so it is important to be mindful of what one consumes mentally. Limiting exposure to negative news, social media comparisons, toxic content, and seeking positive and uplifting content can help maintain a healthier mindset. By consciously utilizing these tips, patients can better cope with the physical and emotional challenges of treatment, adapt to lifestyle changes, and navigate social difficulties with a higher quality of life.

STRESS MANAGEMENT: Developing effective stress management techniques is essential to offset the multitude of stressors related to dialysis. Chronic stress can have a negative impact on the immune system, cardiovascular health, and mental health, which is detrimental to patients. Giving your body the best chance at staying healthy while undergoing dialysis is imperative. Dialysis treatments, along with financial burdens, can be significant sources of stress for patients. The time-consuming nature of dialysis, requiring several hours per day, multiple times a week, and the continuous medical bills can also contribute to increased stress levels. Incorporating deep breathing exercises, staying organized, journaling, and engaging in self-reflection that allows time to identify and address sources of stress can contribute to better mental health. Controlling stress can help patients reduce the psychological and physiological effects of dialysis, leading to a more balanced life.

PRO-TIP

Ongoing research consistently confirms the effectiveness and accessibility of mindfulness practices in reducing stress and anxiety. These practices include strategies such as maintaining a gratitude journal and engaging in breathing exercises. Breathing exercises are not only fast and easy to do, but they are also cost-free. To enhance your ability to practice these techniques and benefit from guided meditations whenever you need them, it may be helpful to utilize resources and apps such as the Insight Timer and Calm App.

Finally, consider incorporating acupuncture into your treatment plan. Acupuncture is a traditional Chinese practice with a long history, and it has been proven to effectively diminish stress, alleviate pain, and improve overall well-being. Acupuncture sessions are pain-free, and patients generally notice positive outcomes after only a few sessions.

SPIRITUAL WELL-BEING

SPIRITUALITY IS THE SACRED practice where we connect with something greater than ourselves, finding a sense of purpose and meaning. It encompasses beliefs, values, and practices that help individuals explore their inner selves, find solace, and seek guidance. Spirituality can play a crucial role in promoting overall well-being, including mental, emotional, and physical health. It enables us to understand life's tests and trials, discover inner strength, and build resilience. In our most difficult times, spirituality can be the silver lining we need by acting as a source of comfort, hope, and peace. When individuals recognize the importance of spirituality, they can develop a deeper sense of self-awareness, find meaning in their experiences, and promote overall well-being. Here are a few ways to nurture your spiritual life:

PRAYER AND SPIRITUAL RITUALS: Prayer is a form of communication with the divine or a higher power, which can be done individually or as part of a religious community. During prayer, you can express gratitude, seek guidance, or simply find comfort in knowing that you are being heard. Prayer is a powerful tool as it allows each patient to feel empowered, which can be fleeting while on dialysis. Prayer also offers a place of comfort and faith, alleviating burdens and fears for many patients.

Rituals are symbolic actions that hold spiritual significance. They can help create a sense of sacredness and provide a structured way to connect with your spirituality. Lighting candles, reciting specific prayers or mantras, using sacred objects, or performing specific gestures or movements may be part of a ritual. Engaging in rituals can promote a sense of connection and belonging, which are crucial during the dialysis process. When engaging in prayer and rituals, it is important to focus on the intention and meaning behind your actions. It is not just about going through the motions but rather about cultivating a genuine connection and reflecting on the purpose of your prayers and rituals to allow for a deepened spiritual experience.

GRATITUDE PRACTICE: Engaging sincerely in a gratitude practice can yield a number of benefits.

Rooting the focus on what is going well, rather than dwelling on what is lacking, leads to a more balanced perspective. When stuck in a dialysis treatment center for so long, it is beneficial for patients to remind themselves of the beauty around them. Journaling is the simplest and easiest way to practice gratitude. By writing down the things you are grateful for, such as a kind gesture, a small accomplishment, or a beautiful sunset, you can help shift your focus to gratitude. Another option is to meditate, focusing on all the things you are grateful for. As you breathe deeply, mentally express gratitude for each object or experience. This will ultimately create a sense of appreciation and contentment. As a bonus, practicing gratitude can increase resilience. It can provide a buffer against negative experiences and help patients bounce back from small adversities. Gratitude practices are personal and can be adapted to fit your personal style and preferences. The key is to regularly engage in activities that help cultivate a mindset of gratitude and appreciation.

1. Connect with your faith or religious community. If you're not part of a religious group, that's okay. Engaging in activities that hold meaning for you, like mentoring children, caring for animals, or volunteering at local libraries, food banks, or community arts centers, can have a positive impact and help you feel a stronger sense of belonging, contentment, and purpose.

2. Spend more time in nature and less time on social media.

3. Focus on hobbies and activities that allow you to be fully present, even if it's just for a short period of time.

4. Reach out to someone you trust, whether it's a spiritual leader, a close friend, or a mental health professional.

Imagine your ideal day without any limitations. Describe in detail how you would spend it and why it would bring you joy.

Resilience is not about being untouched by adversity; it's about using adversity to fuel growth and transformation.

—UNKNOWN

Take a moment to reflect on three things you are grateful for in your life despite the challenges of undergoing dialysis. Consider the support you receive from family and friends, the dedicated healthcare professionals who care for you, or even the advancement in medical technology that make dialysis possible. Express your gratitude for these aspects and how they positively impact your journey.

*Believe in yourself,
take on your challenges
and persevere, but most
importantly know that
you're never alone.*

—MICHELLE OBAMA

GRATITUDE JOURNAL

Describe a dream or aspiration that you have and explain why it is important to you.

____

____

____

____

____

____

*We are hard pressed on
every side, but not crushed;
perplexed, but not in
despair; persecuted, but not
abandoned; struck down,
but not destroyed.*

—2 CORINTHIANS 4:8

GRATITUDE JOURNAL

Think of a small act of kindness or support you have received during your dialysis journey. It could be a caring gesture from a fellow patient, a compassionate nurse or a thoughtful gesture from a loved one. Reflect on how this act made you feel and the impact it had on your overall wellbeing. Take a moment to express your gratitude for this act of kindness and consider the difference it made in your day.

*In the middle of every
difficulty lies opportunity.*

—ALBERT EINSTEIN

Recall a triggering moment when you felt overwhelmed but managed to overcome. Describe the specific steps you took to cope with the situation and any support you sought.

Reflect on how this experience has strengthened your hope and faith and what insights you've gained about yourself.

Reflect on how this experience has strengthened your hope and faith and what insights you've gained about yourself.

____

____

____

____

____

*Never lose hope.
Storms make people stronger
and never last forever."*

—ROY T. BENNETT

Write your personal story exemplifying Radiant Resilience. Detail how you have overcome the challenges and what you are learning from this process.

____

____

____

____

____

*Faith sees the invisible,
believes the unbelievable,
and receives the impossible.*

—CORRIE TEN BOOM

DAILY MAINTENANCE TRACKING

MORNING

AFTERNOON

NIGHT

HELPFUL SUGGESTIONS

- Fully educate yourself about dialysis, including how it works, the different types, and treatment expectations.

- Aim to eat a well-balanced kidney-friendly diet to maintain balanced nutritional levels (e.g., sodium, potassium, phosphorus).

- Manage and understand your medications by organizing them and asking questions about potential interactions with dialysis treatment.

- Recognize signs of infection and any irregularities at the access site. If you notice anything, contact a nurse immediately!

- Traveling is still an option while on dialysis. Depending on the route you take, accommodations can be arranged through your clinic or by traveling with your equipment.

- Be an advocate for your care. Participate in decision-making by asking questions, seeking clarification, and advocating for your needs during appointments.

- Dialysis can cause pruritus due to dry skin and high phosphorus levels. Minimize these symptoms by staying hydrated, moisturizing, and avoiding dairy products.

- If you are on hemodialysis, wear warm clothing and bring a pillow or cushion, as patients tend to get cold and nap during treatments.

- If you are on peritoneal dialysis, make sure all supplies are stocked and connections are made in a safe and sterile manner.

- Keep your fluid intake under 33oz daily, and watch for any signs of swelling in your legs or ankles to avoid fluid overload. (This could result in extra sessions or an extension of treatment time.)

- Remember to keep up with all your appointments outside of your kidney care. Holistic care is key.

- Engage in as much physical activity as possible to maintain your stamina and keep your heart strong.

- Supplements such as B-group vitamins can help prevent deficiencies that may be caused by kidney failure.

- Pursue placement on the transplant list. Your medical team can assist you with the details, and

you can be listed at multiple facilities to increase
your chances of receiving a new kidney.

- Do not be afraid to let your community know that
you are in need. A live donor is a great alternative
to the waiting list, and with the newer guidelines,
cross-matching is possible.

RESOURCES

- Kidney School
  www.kidneyscool.org

- Renal Support Network
  www.rsnhope.org

- American Kidney Fund
  www.kidneyfund.org

- 1+1=LIFE
  www.americantransplantfoundation.org

- National Kidney Foundation
  www.kidney.org

- American Association of Kidney Patients
  www.aakp.org

- Kidney Diet and Nutrition
  Kidneyhood.org

- Life Options Rehabilitation Program
  www.lifeoptions.org

To connect: Email Felecia at weareheartposture@gmail.com
for one on one or group informative sessions.

ACKNOWLEDGMENTS

I WOULD LIKE TO EXPRESS my heartfelt gratitude to those who continue to affirm and care for me throughout this journey.

First and foremost, my deepest thanks to my family, you have been a guiding light in my journey. You have been my foundation, inspiring me to pursue my goals relentlessly. Your belief in me and your support have been invaluable.

I am also grateful to Dr. Olivia Watkins, ND, whose pro tips and expertise have greatly enhanced the quality of this book. Your thoughtful feedback and unwavering support have been a cornerstone during this process.

Finally, I would like to acknowledge my nephew Logan Jace Sullivan. Your memory has been a constant source of inspiration and strength. Although you are no longer with us, your love, wisdom, and encouragement have profoundly influenced this work. I dedicate this book to my best bud, Logan, with all my love.

Resilience: a belief we can influence life events, a tendency to find meaning and purpose in life's turmoil, and a conviction we can learn from positive and negative experiences."

—AMANDA RIPLEY